Brands We Know

Hello Kitty

By Sara Green

Bellwether Media • Minneapolis, MN

Jump into the cockpit and take flight with Pilot books. Your journey will take you on high-energy adventures as you learn about all that is wild, weird, fascinating, and fun!

This edition first published in 2018 by Bellwether Media, Inc.

Library of Congress Cataloging-in-Publication Data

Names: Green, Sara, 1964- author.
Title: Hello Kitty / by Sara Green.
Description: Minneapolis, MN : Bellwether Media, Inc., [2018] | Series:
  Pilot: Brands We Know | Includes bibliographical references and index.
Identifiers: LCCN 2017031298 (print) | LCCN 2017041180 (ebook) | ISBN
  9781626177741 (hardcover : alk. paper) | ISBN 9781681035130 (ebook)
Subjects: LCSH: Hello Kitty (Fictitious character)--Juvenile literature. |
  Character merchandising--Japan--Juveneile literature. | Character
  toys--Japan--Juvenile literature.
Classification: LCC HF5415.17 (ebook) | LCC HF5415.17 .G74 2018 (print) | DDC
  338.4/768872--dc23
LC record available at https://lccn.loc.gov/2017031298

Editor: Betsy Rathburn   Designer: Josh Brink

Printed in the United States of America, North Mankato, MN.

Hello Kitty

Table of Contents

What Is Hello Kitty?

Three friends show their collections to one another. One friend collects stamps. Another shows off her collection of beautiful rocks. The third friend collects something different. She has a shelf filled with Hello Kitty products! A Hello Kitty doll, coin purse, and blanket are among her favorite things. The friends love the adorable Hello Kitty collection!

The Hello Kitty **brand** is known for its cute characters. The most famous is Kitty, a character who looks like a white cat. She was created by a company called Sanrio. The company's **headquarters** is in Tokyo, Japan. There is an enormous variety of Hello Kitty products. The character is found on toys, clothes, and school supplies. Hello Kitty jewelry, **accessories**, and electronics are top sellers. The character has starred in TV programs and videos. There are even theme parks that feature Sanrio characters. Products from this cute brand are sold on every continent except Antarctica. Today, Hello Kitty is worth around $7 billion!

By the Numbers

worth around
$7 billion

more than
70
countries have sold
Hello Kitty products

more than
50,000
Hello Kitty
products available

around
450
different Sanrio
characters

more than
10
video games
feature Hello Kitty

less than
$1
price tag for
first Hello Kitty
product sold

凯蒂猫家园
欢迎您
WELCOME TO
HELLO KITTY PARK

HELLO KITTY PARK

Hello Kitty theme park in Anji County, Zhejiang Province, China

Cute Creations

In 1960, a man named Shintaro Tsuji **founded** the Yamanashi Silk Center Company in Japan. The company made sandals, greeting cards, and small gifts. At that time, people in Japan were buying products with cute designs. Company leaders saw a great opportunity. They began to decorate their products with flowers, fruits, and other designs. The company introduced Strawberry, its first original character, in 1962. More cute characters followed.

Yuko Shimizu

In 1973, the company changed its name to Sanrio. One of Sanrio's most famous characters came to life a year later. A woman named Yuko Shimizu designed a cheerful, nameless character that looked like a white cat. A year later, the character **debuted** on a small coin purse. Above the character was the word "Hello!" The character was an instant hit in Japan. People began calling her Hello Kitty.

Small gift, big smile.
1960s-present Sanrio tagline

Shintaro Tsuji

Sanrio quickly expanded the Hello Kitty line. The character appeared on sewing kits, pencil sharpeners, mugs, and more. Sanrio soon created a life story for the character. Her real name is Kitty White. Her birthday is November 1, and she attends third grade in London. Candy and apple pie are among her favorite foods.

An Unusual Design
Kitty and most of her friends lack mouths. This is meant to make it easier for people to relate to the characters!

You can never have too many friends
current tagline

Papa

Mimmy

Kitty

Mama

Hello Kitty Island Museum and Café in
Jeju, South Korea

Sanrio introduced Kitty's family in 1976. Fans met
Mama, Papa, and Kitty's twin sister, Mimmy. Kitty wears
a red bow on her left ear. Mimmy wears a yellow bow
on her right ear! Fans also met Kitty's grandparents,
Anthony and Margaret. In time, pets joined the family, too.
Charmmykitty is a friendly white cat. She wears the key to
a jewelry box around her neck. A hamster named Sugar
is Charmmykitty's best friend. Charmmykitty has a sister
named Honeycute. She wears two bows and a bracelet
decorated with a heart.

Hello Kitty Craze

Hello Kitty made its debut in the United States in 1976. Two years later, the brand was introduced in Europe. Through the 1980s, even more Hello Kitty products were introduced around the world. The first Hello Kitty **digital** watch was launched in 1980. More than one million were sold! Hello Kitty cameras, towels, and handheld video games also delighted fans.

The 1990s saw a new kind of Hello Kitty craze. The brand had originally been aimed at preteen girls. But teenagers and adults loved it, too. Sanrio expanded the Hello Kitty line to include products for them. Purses, clothing, key rings, and other items aimed at adults flew off store shelves. Sanrio even made Hello Kitty neckties and cell phone cases. **Celebrities** appeared in magazines and on red carpets wearing Hello Kitty fashions. They helped boost the brand's image even more!

Video Game Volleyball

Sanrio released its first Hello Kitty video games in the 1990s. One was called *Sanrio Cup: Pon Pon Volley*. It featured Sanrio characters playing volleyball.

Kitty's group of friends grew over time. Dear Daniel debuted in 1999. He is known for his spiky hair and dancing skills. A bear named Tippy wears a vest and a bow tie. Fifi is a white lamb. She has a tuft of yellow wool on her head. Joey, a mouse, loves to play tag. A raccoon named Tracy makes Kitty laugh!

By 2004, Kitty and her friends had appeared on 50,000 products sold all over the world. The products have always come in a wide range of prices. Many items, including stickers, pencils, and paper plates, cost a few dollars or less. However, some Hello Kitty items cost much more. Kids can drive Hello Kitty cars designed just for them. Adults can wear Hello Kitty jewelry made with diamonds and other gems. A Hello Kitty doll covered in crystals is one of the most expensive Hello Kitty items in the world. It is worth more than $150,000!

The Friendship Party

Kitty ran for President of the United States in 2012 and 2016 as a member of the Friendship Party. This pretend party's goal was to spread happiness, friendship, and fun.

Meet Hello Kitty's Friends!

Character	Animal
Dear Daniel	cat
Fifi	sheep
Jodie	dog
Joey	mouse
Mory	mole
Rorry	squirrel
Thomas	bear
Tim and Tammy	monkeys
Tippy	bear cub
Tracy	raccoon

Jodie

Dear Daniel

Fifi

Tracy

Rorry

Hello Kitty Today

Today, new Hello Kitty products debut regularly. Hello Kitty clothes and makeup are top-selling products. People can also buy Hello Kitty suitcases, tents, and sleeping bags. Sanrio often **licenses** the character to other companies. McDonald's has included Hello Kitty toys in its Happy Meals. Hello Kitty recently teamed up with the Strawberry Shortcake brand. Kitty and Strawberry Shortcake now appear together on totes, lunch boxes, and other products.

Hello Kitty Hospital

A Hello Kitty hospital opened in 2008 in Taiwan. Rooms are decorated with Hello Kitty images. Patients sleep on Hello Kitty sheets, and nurses wear uniforms with Hello Kitty designs.

EVA Air Hello Kitty airplane

Kitty appears in other fun places, too. An airline called EVA Air uses planes painted with Hello Kitty designs. Passengers check in at a gate decorated with Hello Kitty images. Inside the plane, Kitty appears on pillows, napkins, and safety cards. Even the food has a Hello Kitty theme!

Since 2014, a Hello Kitty food truck has traveled to cities across the United States. Customers can buy Hello Kitty treats, T-shirts, and bows. In 2017, a Hello Kitty café opened in California. It serves cookies, cakes, and other treats. The Hello Kitty brand is everywhere!

Fans and Friendship

Over time, Hello Kitty's message of friendship and happiness has led Kitty into new roles. Kitty was named a children's **ambassador** for **UNICEF** in the United States in 1983. About a **decade** later, she held the same title in Japan. Kitty became Japan's ambassador of **tourism** to China and Hong Kong in 2008. It was the first time Japan had named a pretend character to the role. Kitty appeared on a web site that gave information about Japanese attractions, restaurants, and shopping areas.

Hello Kitty becomes ambassador of tourism

Hello Kitty's 40th birthday celebration

In 2013, Hello Kitty started a **campaign** called Share a Hug with Hello Kitty for the brand's 40th birthday. Kitty appeared at special events around the world to give hugs and spread fun and friendship. Sanrio kept track of each hug on its Global Hug Report. The next year, Hello Kitty participated in **Macaron** Day in France and Japan. The event helped raise money for organizations that help children fight diseases.

Playing For A Cause

Members of an online game called *Hello Kitty Online* donated more than 500,000 items to people hit by an earthquake in Haiti in 2010.

Hello Kitty fans enjoy celebrating their favorite character. The first Hello Kitty Con was held in Los Angeles, California, in 2014. This four-day **conference** featured Hello Kitty displays, workshops, and activities. Many people dressed up as their favorite Sanrio characters. The event drew 25,000 people from all over the world. Even singer Katy Perry attended!

Hello Kitty's Supercute Friendship Festival toured the United States in 2015. The festival was similar to Hello Kitty Con. It featured performances by Kitty and her friends. Participants also enjoyed taking photos and wearing costumes!

Sports fans celebrate Hello Kitty, too. Some baseball teams, like the Milwaukee Brewers and San Francisco Giants, have had Hello Kitty nights. Fans can go home with a Hello Kitty T-shirt or tote bag. The LA Clippers basketball team also hosted a Hello Kitty night. Fans received a Hello Kitty blanket. Hello Kitty brings smiles and friendship to people everywhere!

San Francisco Giants game

Coming Soon

A Hello Kitty movie is set to hit the big screen in 2019. Fans must wait to see what the movie is about. But they can count on seeing some of their favorite Sanrio characters in action!

Hello Kitty Timeline

1960
Shintaro Tsuji founds the Yamanashi Silk Center Company in Japan

1981
Hello Kitty makes her big-screen debut in *Kitty and Mimmy's New Umbrella*

1974
Yuko Shimizu designs a white cat character

1976
Hello Kitty debuts in the United States

1990
Sanrio Puroland theme park opens in Tokyo, Japan

1973
Company name is changed to Sanrio

1980
The Hello Kitty digital watch is launched

1983
UNICEF gives Hello Kitty the title of UNICEF Special Friend of Children in the United States

1975
The character debuts on a vinyl coin purse and is called Hello Kitty by fans

1999
Dear Daniel is
introduced

2005
The first Hello Kitty
airplane debuts

2009
Hello Kitty Online
is launched

2014
Hello Kitty Con is
held in California

2007
Hello Kitty debuts
in the Macy's
Thanksgiving Day
Parade

2017
A Hello Kitty café
opens in California

Glossary

accessories—things added to something else to make it more useful or attractive

ambassador—someone who acts as a representative of a country or special activity

brand—a category of products all made by the same company

campaign—an organized action or event aimed to achieve a particular goal

celebrities—famous people

conference—a formal meeting for people interested in the same topic

debuted—was introduced for the first time

decade—a period of ten years

digital—related to electronic or computerized technology

founded—created a company

headquarters—a company's main office

licenses—allows the use or sale of a property, often in exchange for money

macaron—a round, brightly colored sandwich cookie with a sweet filling

tourism—the business of traveling to visit other places

UNICEF—United Nations Children's Fund; UNICEF is an organization that helps children in need.

To Learn More

AT THE LIBRARY

Brown, Peggy, and Nate Lovett. *The Everything Girls Super Cute Kawaii Fun Book*. Avon, Mass.: Adams Media, 2015.

Gitlin, Marty. *Japan*. Minneapolis, Minn.: Bellwether Media, 2018.

Green, Sara. *Pokémon*. Minneapolis, Minn.: Bellwether Media, 2018.

ON THE WEB

Learning more about
Hello Kitty is as easy as 1, 2, 3.

1. Go to www.factsurfer.com.

2. Enter "Hello Kitty" into the search box.

3. Click the "Surf" button and you
   will see a list of related web sites.

With factsurfer.com, finding more information
is just a click away.

Index